HOW TO USE A YARN BALL WINDER

Unlocking the Secrets of Yarn Winding for Crafters

Fitzpatrick J. Thompkins

Table of Contents

Introduction

In the quaint town of Weaverly, nestled between rolling hills and whispering forests, there was a small, but bustling, yarn shop known to all as The Knitting Nest. Its owner, Eleanor, was a master knitter whose skills were the talk of the town and beyond. Her secret, she often whispered with a wink, wasn't just in her decades of experience but in a tool so valuable, yet so overlooked by many: the yarn ball winder.

One crisp autumn morning, a young man named Thomas entered The Knitting Nest with a look of determination. He had recently discovered the joys of knitting but found himself constantly battling tangled yarn and uneven balls that made his knitting experience less than peaceful.

"I've heard you have a secret weapon that can turn my knitting woes into wonders," Thomas said, eyeing the colorful displays of yarn.

Eleanor smiled, leading him to a shelf that held a small, yet promising book titled "How to Use a Yarn Ball Winder." As she handed it to him, she began to tell the tale of how this guide had transformed her craft.

"This isn't just a book; it's a journey into mastering the art of yarn preparation," Eleanor explained. "Within its pages, you'll discover not just the mechanics of using a yarn ball winder but the soulful art of turning skeins into neat, ready-to-use balls of yarn."

Thomas was intrigued as Eleanor continued, describing the contents of the book. She spoke of chapters that detailed the setup of a yarn ball winder, the basic operation, and even advanced techniques for different types of yarns. She told tales of the creative uses beyond yarn, maintenance tips to keep the winder in top condition, and how to troubleshoot common issues.

"But why this book?" Thomas asked, genuinely curious. "Can't I just figure it out on my own?"

Eleanor leaned closer, her eyes sparkling with wisdom. "This book isn't just about avoiding the frustration of tangles or the satisfaction of creating perfect yarn balls. It's about embracing a tool that elevates your crafting, saving you time and allowing you to focus on the joy of creation. It's written with the beginner in mind but filled with insights that even experienced knitters will find invaluable."

As Thomas flipped through the pages, he could see the detailed illustrations, the step-by-step guides, and the passionate words that made the process seem so simple, yet so profound. He realized that this book was more than a manual; it was a gateway to a deeper understanding of his craft.

"By the time you reach the conclusion," Eleanor said, "you'll not only know how to use a yarn ball winder but why it's an indispensable part of your knitting toolkit. You'll have more than just skills; you'll have confidence."

Thomas purchased the book without hesitation, eager to embark on this new chapter of his knitting journey. As days turned into weeks, the once daunting piles of yarn became neatly wound balls of potential, and Thomas's creations flourished like never before.

And so, in the heart of Weaverly, through the pages of a seemingly simple guide, a new artisan was born, his craft forever changed by the wisdom contained in "How to Use a Yarn Ball Winder." It wasn't just about making things easier; it was about making them better, with each turn of the winder weaving not just yarn, but also a deeper connection to the craft itself.

Purpose of a Yarn Ball Winder

A yarn ball winder is an essential tool for knitters, crocheters, and fiber artists, designed to transform skeins or hanks of yarn into neat, compact balls that are easier to work with and store. The purpose of a yarn ball winder in the crafting process cannot be overstated, as it directly impacts efficiency, organization, and even the enjoyment of the crafting experience.

The traditional method of winding yarn by hand is time-consuming and often results in uneven balls that can roll away or tangle. A yarn ball winder addresses these issues by creating uniform balls that pull smoothly from the center, eliminating the frustration of knots and tangles. This not only saves time but also reduces the wear and tear on the yarn that can occur when it is repeatedly pulled and untangled.

Moreover, using a yarn ball winder helps in maintaining an organized crafting space. The compact balls are easier to store and sort through, allowing crafters to quickly find the color or type of yarn they need without sifting through tangled heaps. This level of organization is particularly beneficial for those who work on multiple projects simultaneously or who have limited storage space.

The aesthetic appeal of neatly wound yarn balls also adds to the overall crafting experience. There is a certain satisfaction in seeing a collection of uniformly wound yarn balls, ready for use. This visual organization can also spark creativity, making it easier for crafters to plan new projects and color combinations.

Furthermore, a yarn ball winder is instrumental in preserving the quality of the yarn. When wound properly, the yarn is protected from stretching, fraying, or becoming misshapen, which can happen when yarn is stored in a loose or tangled state. This preservation of quality ensures that each project starts with the best possible material, contributing to the final look and durability of the crafted item.

Learning how to use a yarn ball winder effectively is a skill that enhances the crafting process from start to finish. The guide "How to Use a Yarn Ball Winder" provides invaluable insights into not just the operation of the winder but also tips for selecting the right winder for one's needs, advanced winding techniques, and maintenance advice to keep the winder in optimal condition. By mastering the use of a yarn ball winder, crafters can spend less time preparing their materials and more time on the enjoyable aspects of creating handmade items.

In essence, the purpose of a yarn ball winder transcends its simple function. It is a tool that enriches the crafting experience, fostering a sense of satisfaction and creativity. It allows crafters to focus on their passion with fewer interruptions, making it a worthwhile investment for anyone serious about knitting, crocheting, or working with yarn in any capacity.

Benefits of Using a Yarn Ball Winder

Using a yarn ball winder comes with a myriad of benefits that enhance the crafting experience for knitters, crocheters, and artisans alike. This simple yet transformative tool efficiently turns skeins or hanks of yarn into neat, compact balls, streamlining the preparation process and enabling a smoother workflow. One of the primary advantages is the significant time saved. Manually winding yarn can be a slow, tedious process, but with a yarn ball winder, what used to take hours can now be accomplished in minutes. This newfound efficiency allows crafters to dedicate more time to the creative aspects of their projects, making the entire process more enjoyable and productive.

Beyond just saving time, the consistency and uniformity provided by a yarn ball winder improve the overall quality of craft projects. Yarn wound into tight, even balls ensures uniform tension throughout the knitting or crocheting process, reducing the likelihood of encountering knots or tangled messes that can interrupt workflow and affect the finished product. This uniform tension is crucial for achieving consistent stitch sizes, which is essential for projects that demand precision and uniformity.

Another benefit lies in the space-saving aspect of using a yarn ball winder. Yarn balls created by this tool are compact and stackable, making them easier to store and organize. This is particularly valuable for those with limited storage space or for crafters who manage large quantities of yarn. Efficient storage not only helps in maintaining a clutter-free workspace but also in preserving the yarn's quality by preventing tangles and keeping it clean.

Furthermore, the yarn ball winder promotes a more ergonomic crafting experience. Winding yarn by hand can strain the wrists and arms, leading to fatigue or even repetitive strain injuries over time. Using a yarn ball winder minimizes this risk, providing a more comfortable and sustainable crafting practice. This aspect is especially beneficial for those who knit or crochet regularly or for extended periods.

The versatility of a yarn ball winder also extends to its ability to handle various types of yarn, from delicate lace to bulky wool. This adaptability makes it an invaluable tool for artisans working with a wide range of materials. Additionally, winders can create balls that pull from the outside or the center, offering flexibility in how the yarn is used and facilitating an easier start to any project.

In the realm of creative endeavors, a yarn ball winder enriches the crafting experience not only through practical benefits but also by nurturing the joy and satisfaction derived from engaging in textile arts. It empowers crafters to focus more on the creative process and less on the preparatory steps, elevating the quality of their work and their overall enjoyment of the craft.

In relation to learning "How to Use a Yarn Ball Winder," understanding these benefits underscores the importance of incorporating this tool into one's crafting repertoire. It's not just about learning a new skill but about embracing a tool that can significantly enhance the efficiency, quality, and pleasure of yarn crafting activities. As such, the investment in a yarn ball winder, coupled with the knowledge of how to effectively use it, becomes an invaluable asset for anyone passionate about knitting, crocheting, or any form of yarn art.

Chapter: 1 Understanding Your Yarn Ball Winder

Parts of a Yarn Ball Winder

Understanding the various components of a yarn ball winder is crucial for anyone looking to master its use. A yarn ball winder is a simple, yet ingeniously designed tool that serves the primary function of turning skeins or hanks of yarn into neat, compact balls. Each part of the yarn ball winder plays a significant role in this process, ensuring efficiency and ease of use.

At the heart of the yarn ball winder is the spindle or cone. This is the central part around which the yarn is wound, transforming it into a ball. The spindle's shape and size are specifically designed to accommodate yarn as it wraps around, allowing for a tight and even winding. The smooth surface of the spindle also helps in preventing the yarn from snagging or getting damaged during the winding process.

Attached to the spindle is the crank handle. This is the part that users manually operate to wind the yarn. Turning the crank handle rotates the spindle, and as the handle turns, the yarn is drawn from the skein or hank and wound onto the spindle. The ease of movement and ergonomic design of the crank handle are essential for a comfortable winding experience, especially during extended use.

Another critical component is the yarn guide, which is usually a metal arm with an eyelet through which the yarn is threaded before it reaches the spindle. The yarn guide ensures that the yarn feeds onto the spindle at the correct angle and tension, promoting even distribution across the spindle. This part is adjustable on many models, allowing users to modify the tension and angle according to the type of yarn or the desired tightness of the yarn ball.

The clamp or base is what secures the yarn ball winder to a table or any stable surface. It's designed to hold the winder firmly in place during use, preventing movement that could disrupt the winding process. The strength and stability provided by the clamp are vital, especially since a good grip is necessary to handle the tension and motion of winding effectively.

Some yarn ball winders may also feature a tension arm or adjustment settings. These components allow for finer control over the tension of the yarn as it winds. Adjusting the tension is crucial for different yarn thicknesses and textures to ensure the yarn ball is neither too loose nor too tightly wound. This flexibility enhances the functionality of the yarn ball winder, making it suitable for a wide range of yarn types.

Lastly, many winders come with a built-in counter, which helps track the amount of yarn wound. This feature is particularly beneficial for projects requiring precise lengths of yarn, allowing crafters to measure and cut exact amounts without the need for additional tools.

Understanding these components and their functions is not just about operating the yarn ball winder efficiently; it's about harnessing the tool's full potential to enhance one's crafting experience. Whether for personal projects or professional use, a deep understanding of the parts of a yarn ball winder, as outlined in "How to Use a Yarn Ball Winder," empowers users to prepare their yarn with precision and ease, paving the way for smoother, more enjoyable crafting sessions.

Types of Yarn Ball Winders

In the world of yarn crafting, the yarn ball winder is an indispensable tool that transforms skeins and hanks into neat, workable balls of yarn. Understanding the different types of yarn ball winders can significantly enhance your crafting experience, enabling you to choose the perfect winder for your specific needs. This understanding is crucial, especially when learning how to use a yarn ball winder effectively.

Yarn ball winders come in various designs and capacities, catering to different preferences, yarn types, and project sizes. The two primary categories are manual and electric winders, each with its unique features and benefits.

Manual Yarn Ball Winders are the most commonly used type among hobbyists and professionals alike. Operated by a hand crank, these winders give the user complete control over the winding speed and tension. They are typically made from durable materials like plastic and metal and come in sizes that can handle anywhere from 4 to 10 ounces of yarn at a time. Manual winders are appreciated for their portability, ease of use, and affordability. They require no power source, making them ideal for crafters on the go or those who prefer a more hands-on approach to yarn winding.

Electric Yarn Ball Winders offer a higher level of efficiency and convenience. Powered by electricity, these winders can wind yarn faster than manual models, making them a favorite for those who work with large quantities of yarn or who wish to save time. Electric winders often feature variable speed settings, allowing users to adjust the winding pace according to the yarn type or personal preference. While they tend to be more expensive and less portable than manual winders, their speed and ease of use make them an excellent investment for serious knitters and crocheters.

Within these two main categories, yarn ball winders can also vary based on their construction material, capacity, and additional features. Some winders are designed with special features to accommodate different yarn weights, from delicate lace to bulky wool, ensuring that the winder can handle the specific needs of various projects. Others include built-in yarn tensioners and guides, which help maintain consistent tension and prevent tangling or snarls during the winding process.

When choosing a yarn ball winder, consider the types of projects you typically work on, the volume of yarn you need to wind, and your personal preferences in terms of manual versus electric operation. For those just starting out or who work on smaller projects, a compact manual winder may be sufficient. However, for those who find themselves constantly winding yarn or tackling larger projects, investing in an electric model might save time and effort in the long run.

In learning how to use a yarn ball winder, it's essential to familiarize yourself with the specific type you have chosen. Each winder will come with its own set of instructions and best practices, from setting up and threading the yarn to winding and removing the finished ball. Understanding these nuances will ensure that you get the most out of your yarn ball winder, regardless of the type, enhancing both the efficiency and enjoyment of your crafting experience.

Choosing the Right Yarn Ball Winder for Your Needs

Selecting the appropriate yarn ball winder can markedly improve your crafting experience, whether you're a novice or a seasoned knitter or crocheter. When choosing the right yarn ball winder, it's crucial to consider several key factors that align with your specific needs and preferences.

The first consideration should be the type of yarn ball winder, which generally falls into two categories: manual and electric. Manual winders are operated by a crank and require physical effort to wind the yarn. They are typically more affordable and portable, making them suitable for those who wind yarn occasionally or are looking for a budget-friendly option. On the other hand, electric yarn ball winders are powered by a motor, requiring minimal physical effort. They are ideal for those who wind large quantities of yarn regularly, as they can save a significant amount of time and reduce manual labor.

The capacity of the yarn ball winder is another crucial aspect. Winders vary in the amount of yarn they can handle at one time, from small units that hold about 3-4 ounces of yarn per winding, to larger models that can accommodate up to 16 ounces or more. Selecting a winder with the right capacity depends on your typical yarn usage. For personal use, a smaller winder may suffice, but for more extensive projects or professional use, a larger capacity winder is more practical.

Durability and construction quality are also vital. A well-built yarn ball winder should be sturdy and stable during operation. Models made with strong materials, such as metal, tend to last longer and perform better than those made predominantly of plastic. Checking the quality of the gears, which are essential for smooth operation, is also recommended. Metal gears generally offer better durability and smoother performance compared to plastic gears, which might wear down or break more easily.

Ease of use is another important factor. A good yarn ball winder should be easy to set up, operate, and maintain. Features such as adjustable tension, easy clamping to various surfaces, and clear instructions enhance the usability of the winder. For those who enjoy winding different types of yarn, look for a winder that can handle everything from delicate threads to thick, chunky yarns without causing damage or tangling.

Compatibility with other tools you might be using, such as yarn swifts, is also something to consider. Some yarn ball winders can be used in conjunction with a swift to handle skeins more effectively, turning the winding process into a smoother, faster, and more enjoyable task.

Lastly, consider the reviews and recommendations from other crafters. Learning from the experiences of others can provide insight into the reliability and efficiency of different models and brands. Craft forums, product review sites, and online crafting communities are valuable resources for gathering this information.

In relation to learning "How to Use a Yarn Ball Winder," choosing the right model is foundational. Understanding the different types of winders, their capacities, construction qualities, and ease of use not only aids in making an informed purchase but also ensures that you get the most out of your yarn crafting experience. A well-chosen yarn ball winder complements your skills and needs, making the entire process from winding to knitting or crocheting smoother and more enjoyable.

Chapter: 2 Setting Up Your Yarn Ball Winder

Unboxing and Assembling

Unboxing and assembling a yarn ball winder is a straightforward process that sets the foundation for efficient and enjoyable yarn crafting. When you first receive your yarn ball winder, the package will typically include the main winder body, a table clamp, and possibly additional spindles or gears, depending on the model. Here's a step-by-step guide to ensure a proper setup:

Step 1: Unboxing

Carefully open the box and remove all parts. It's important to keep the packaging material until you confirm that the winder is fully functional and no parts are missing or damaged. Lay out the components on a clean, flat surface. You should find the main winding unit, a clamp to secure the winder to a table or shelf, and often an instruction manual. Inspect each piece for any signs of damage during shipping.

Step 2: Familiarizing With Parts

Take a moment to familiarize yourself with each part of the winder. The main body usually consists of a crank handle that you will turn to wind the yarn, a yarn guide that directs the yarn smoothly onto the spindle, and the spindle or bobbin itself where the yarn will be wound. The clamp is used to secure the device to a stable surface.

Step 3: Choosing a Suitable Location

Select a sturdy, flat surface like a table or a desk for the yarn ball winder. Ensure the space is ample enough to accommodate the movement of the winder and the yarn. The surface should also be near where you store your yarn for easy access.

Step 4: Attaching the Clamp

Fix the clamp to your chosen surface, making sure it's tight and secure. Most clamps have a protective coating to prevent damage to your furniture but check to make sure it is positioned correctly. The winder should sit firmly and not wobble or move during operation.

Step 5: Assembling the Winder

Attach the main body of the winder to the clamp according to the instructions provided. This usually involves sliding the winder onto the clamp and tightening it so that it stays in place. Ensure that the winder is positioned so that the crank handle is easily reachable and that there is enough room to turn it comfortably.

Step 6: Installing the Yarn Guide

If the yarn guide isn't already attached, you will need to install it. This part guides the yarn from your skein to the spindle in a

smooth manner to prevent tangles and ensures even winding.
Position it so that it aligns with the spindle and secures it as
directed in the manual.

Step 7: Testing the Winder

Before you start using the winder for your projects, it's wise to test
it with an inexpensive yarn or waste yarn. Attach the yarn to the
spindle, and gently start turning the crank handle to see how the
yarn feeds through the guide and winds onto the spindle. Adjust
the tension and position of the guide as needed to achieve a
smooth, tight wind.

Step 8: Consulting the Manual

Throughout the process, refer to the manufacturer's manual for
specific instructions or troubleshooting tips. Manuals often
contain useful information on the optimal operation of your
specific model, which can enhance your winding experience.

Once assembled, your yarn ball winder is ready to use. Proper
setup not only ensures the longevity of the tool but also enhances
your yarn crafting, making it a more pleasurable and productive
experience. Taking the time to set up your yarn ball winder
correctly will save you time and frustration in your knitting or
crocheting projects, allowing you to focus more on creativity and
less on untangling yarn.

Mounting Your Yarn Ball Winder

Mounting your yarn ball winder correctly is a crucial step in setting up your crafting station, ensuring that you can efficiently and effectively wind yarn into neat, usable balls. The process of mounting your yarn ball winder involves a few straightforward steps, but getting it right enhances your overall experience and contributes to smoother, more reliable operation.

First, choose a suitable location for your yarn ball winder. This should be a flat, stable surface such as a sturdy table or desk. It's important to have enough space not only for the winder itself but also for the movement of the yarn and your arms as you operate the device. Adequate lighting is also crucial, as it helps you monitor the yarn's tension and progress as it winds.

Once you have identified the right spot, inspect your yarn ball winder for a clamp or mounting mechanism. This is typically located at the base of the winder and is used to secure the device to the edge of your chosen surface. The clamp should be adjustable to accommodate different thicknesses of tabletops. Make sure that the surface you choose is not too thick for the clamp's maximum extension, nor too thin that it doesn't provide a secure hold.

To mount the winder, open the clamp and position it at the edge of the table or surface. It's advisable to mount the winder so that it is slightly overhanging the edge of the surface. This positioning allows the winder to rotate freely without any obstruction from the table. Once in position, tighten the clamp until the winder is securely attached and does not wobble or shift when touched. It's essential that the winder is mounted firmly to prevent any movement during operation, as this could lead to unevenly wound yarn or, worse, damage to the winder or the yarn.

After securing the yarn ball winder, test the stability by gently pulling on it to ensure it does not move or detach from the surface. This test is important as it ensures that the winder will stay in place under the tension of winding yarn. Additionally, check that the winder's crank turns smoothly and that the yarn guide moves freely. Any resistance in these parts may need addressing before you start winding yarn.

Now that your yarn ball winder is mounted correctly, you can proceed to thread the yarn and begin winding. Properly mounting your yarn ball winder not only facilitates a seamless yarn winding process but also prevents strain on your hands and wrists, making your crafting sessions more enjoyable and productive.

In the context of learning how to use a yarn ball winder, understanding how to mount it properly is fundamental. This knowledge ensures that every winding session starts on the right note, with a stable setup that supports the efficient transformation of tangled hanks or skeins into tidy, ready-to-use balls of yarn. Ensuring your yarn ball winder is correctly installed is an investment in both the longevity of the tool and the quality of your crafting projects.

Safety Precautions and Tips

When setting up and using a yarn ball winder, adhering to safety precautions is crucial to prevent accidents and ensure a smooth, efficient operation. These safety tips are essential not only for protecting the user but also for maintaining the longevity and effectiveness of the device.

First and foremost, it's important to select an appropriate area for setting up the yarn ball winder. The surface should be stable, flat, and free of any clutter. An unstable surface can cause the winder to move unexpectedly during operation, which can lead to improper winding or damage to the yarn and the winder itself. Additionally, ensure the area is well-lit, which helps in accurately threading the yarn and monitoring the winding process to avoid potential hazards.

Before attaching the yarn ball winder to any surface, check the clamping mechanism to ensure it is in good working condition. The clamp should be securely fastened to a table or a shelf to prevent the winder from slipping or becoming detached. This is crucial, as a loose winder can not only disrupt the winding process but also pose a risk of injury.

It's also important to inspect the yarn ball winder for any damaged or worn-out parts before use. Frayed gears, a loose spindle, or a cracked body can affect the functionality and safety of the winder. Replace any damaged parts immediately to avoid accidents or further damage to the machine. Regular maintenance, such as cleaning the winder to remove lint and yarn fibers that accumulate over time, also plays a vital role in safe operation.

When using the yarn ball winder, keep your fingers away from the gears and other moving parts. The winding mechanism can easily catch loose clothing, jewelry, or even hair, which can lead to injuries. It's advisable to wear fitted clothing and to keep long hair tied back while operating the winder.

Additionally, operate the yarn ball winder at a reasonable speed. Although some winders can handle fast winding, starting at a slower pace allows for more control and reduces the chances of the yarn tangling or snapping. Once you become more accustomed to the winder's operation, you can gradually increase the speed as appropriate.

If children are present, it is essential to supervise their interaction with the yarn ball winder. While it can be a fun and educational tool, the moving parts can be hazardous. Explain to children the proper use of the winder, and always supervise them closely if they are participating in the winding process.

Finally, storing the yarn ball winder correctly when not in use is also a part of safety precautions. Keep it in a safe, dry place out of reach of children and away from any heat sources. Ensuring the winder is properly stored not only keeps it safe from accidental damage but also extends its lifespan.

By following these safety precautions and tips when setting up and using a yarn ball winder, crafters can enjoy a seamless, productive, and safe crafting experience. These practices ensure that the focus remains on creativity and enjoyment, minimizing the risks and maximizing the benefits of using this valuable tool.

Chapter: 3 Basic Operation of a Yarn Ball Winder

Preparing Your Yarn

Preparing your yarn properly is a crucial step in the basic operation of a yarn ball winder and significantly impacts the effectiveness and ease of the winding process. The goal is to ensure that the yarn transitions smoothly from its original form—whether a skein, hank, or another type of bundle—into a neatly wound ball that is easy to use for knitting or crocheting.

The first step in preparing your yarn involves understanding the form it comes in. Yarn often arrives in hanks, which are loose loops that need to be unwound before use. Begin by carefully untwisting the hank and finding the ends. Place the hank over a swift—an adjustable tool that holds the loops of yarn in place—and expand the swift to maintain gentle tension on the hank. This setup prevents the yarn from tangling as it is unwound.

Once the hank is mounted on the swift, locate the end of the yarn that will feed into the ball winder. It's crucial to start with the correct end to avoid knots and snags during winding. One end is usually tied off to keep the hank together during packaging; this should be untied and the yarn end freed. If the yarn resists when you begin to pull, try the other end to find the one that unravels freely.

Next, thread the loose end of the yarn through the guide on the yarn ball winder. This typically involves feeding the yarn through one or more metal eyes or hooks that help direct the yarn smoothly onto the winder's spindle. The initial setup should be secure to prevent the yarn from slipping out during winding. A small knot or a twist can be used to anchor the yarn's end to the winder's core or spindle, ensuring it stays in place as the winding begins.

Once the yarn is securely attached and correctly threaded through the guide mechanisms, check the path from the swift to the winder to ensure there are no obstructions or sharp angles that could cause the yarn to snag or break. The yarn should flow freely from the swift, through the guide, and onto the winder. Ensure that the yarn moves smoothly without any tension that could distort the fibers or cause uneven winding.

Begin winding slowly, using a steady pace to ensure the yarn wraps neatly around the spindle of the ball winder. As you wind, keep an eye on the tension; it should be tight enough to create a firm ball, but not so tight that it stretches the yarn. An even tension helps produce a ball that maintains its shape and dispenses easily during subsequent use.

Adjust the speed and tension as necessary, based on how the yarn feeds through the swift and winder. Some thicker or textured yarns might require a slower winding speed to prevent tangling or snagging. On the other hand, smoother, thinner yarns can often be wound more quickly.

Finally, as you approach the end of the yarn, slow down the winding process to ensure the final wraps are secure and do not unravel. Once the yarn is fully wound, carefully remove the ball from the winder, making sure to secure the loose end so it doesn't unravel during storage or use.

By following these detailed steps in preparing your yarn, you ensure that your yarn ball winder operates efficiently, delivering neatly wound yarn balls that are easy to store and use, enhancing your overall crafting experience. This thorough preparation not only saves time and reduces frustration but also contributes to the quality and enjoyment of your knitting or crocheting projects.

Threading the Yarn Through the Winder

Threading the yarn through the winder is a crucial step in the basic operation of a yarn ball winder, and mastering this technique ensures a smooth start and finish to your winding session. When you first approach this task, it's important to ensure that your winder is securely attached to a stable, flat surface, typically at the edge of a table or a bench. This positioning allows for easy access and operation.

To begin, select your yarn skein or hank. If you're working with a hank, it must be untwisted and placed on a swift. The swift holds the yarn taut and spins freely, which is essential for an even feed into the ball winder. If you're starting with a skein, ensure it's free from knots and tangles to avoid interruptions during the winding process.

Once your yarn is ready, locate the end of the yarn that will feed smoothly into the winder. This is typically an outer end, as pulling from the inside can cause the skein or hank to collapse and tangle. Take this end and thread it through the metal yarn guide on the ball winder. This guide is crucial as it helps maintain the yarn's tension and alignment as it enters the winder.

After passing through the guide, the yarn end must then be attached to the winder's bobbin or spindle. Many winders have a small slot or notch on the top of the spindle; this is where you securely fasten the yarn. Insert the yarn end into this slot, ensuring it's snug enough that it won't slip free during winding but not so tight as to prevent easy unwinding later. This initial securing of the yarn is what guarantees a tidy, compact ball at the end of the process.

Now, you're ready to begin winding. Start turning the handle of the winder slowly, maintaining an even pace. As you crank the handle, the yarn will begin to wrap around the spindle, starting at the bottom and gradually working its way up to form a neat, even ball. The tension guide plays a pivotal role during this phase, as it prevents the yarn from becoming too loose or too tightly wound, both of which can affect the quality of your finished ball.

It's essential to keep an eye on the yarn feeding from the swift or skein into the winder during this process. Make sure there's no undue stress or pulling at the yarn source, as this can cause snags or breaks. Adjust the tension as needed to ensure a smooth feed. If you notice any irregularities in tension or alignment, stop winding, address the issue, and then resume.

As you approach the end of your skein or hank, slow down the winding process. This careful finishing ensures that the final wraps are just as even as the first, preventing the yarn ball from unraveling or becoming too loose once removed from the winder.

Finally, once all the yarn is wound, carefully remove the yarn ball from the spindle. You might need to cut the yarn connecting to the remains of the skein or hank if any, and then tuck the loose end under a few strands on the surface of the yarn ball to secure it.

The successful threading and winding of yarn through a yarn ball winder not only save time but also enhance the pleasure and productivity of knitting or crocheting projects. By efficiently transforming loose yarn into user-friendly balls, the winder allows crafters to maintain focus on their creative endeavors without interruption, ensuring a satisfying and fruitful crafting experience.

Starting the Winding Process

Starting the winding process with a yarn ball winder is a straightforward task that, once mastered, becomes a quick and essential step in the preparation of yarn for knitting, crocheting, or other fiber arts. To begin, it's important to first ensure that the yarn ball winder is securely mounted on a stable surface. This can typically be done via a built-in clamp that attaches to a table or desk edge. Ensuring stability is crucial as it prevents the winder from moving or tipping during use, which could cause uneven winding or damage to the yarn.

Once the winder is set up, the next step is to prepare the yarn. If you're starting with a skein, it should be unwound and placed into a loose pile or ideally, on a yarn swift, which rotates to release the yarn smoothly without tangling. This helps maintain an even tension and feed as the yarn is wound into a ball. For those using hanks of yarn, it's essential to first untwist the hank and lay it out in a large circle, again ideally placing it on a yarn swift.

The actual winding begins by securing the end of the yarn to the yarn ball winder. Most winders have a small slot or notch on the top of the spindle where the yarn end can be inserted. This initial attachment is critical as it holds the yarn in place and prevents it from slipping as the winding process begins. After securing the yarn, gently tug on it to ensure it is firmly in place and will not pull free once winding commences.

To start winding, slowly turn the handle of the yarn ball winder with one hand while the other hand guides the yarn. It's important to maintain a consistent speed and tension on the yarn as it feeds into the winder. Starting slowly helps you control the yarn and avoid too loose or too tight winding, both of which can affect how the yarn pulls during your crafting project. As you turn the handle, the yarn will begin to wrap around the spindle, gradually building into a larger ball. The winding should continue in this consistent, controlled manner.

As the ball grows, periodically check to ensure that the yarn is not tangling or catching. If the yarn appears to be twisting excessively or forming loops, it may be necessary to adjust your speed or the tension with which you are guiding the yarn. This can happen if the yarn swift is turning too quickly or too slowly in relation to the speed of the winding. Adjustments might be minor, such as slightly increasing or decreasing the speed of your handle turns, or more significant, such as stopping to untangle a knot or reposition the yarn on the swift.

Continue winding until all the yarn is transferred from the skein or hank onto the winder, forming a neat, compact ball. When reaching the end of the yarn, detach it from the swift or pile and secure the free end under several layers of the yarn on the ball to prevent it from unraveling. This last step is important as it ensures the yarn ball remains tidy and ready for use.

The winding process, when done correctly, results in a yarn ball that is easy to use, with yarn that feeds smoothly and is free from knots and tangles. This preparation greatly enhances the crafting experience, allowing for seamless knitting or crocheting, and it all begins with mastering the basic operation of a yarn ball winder.

Adjusting Tension and Speed

Adjusting the tension and speed of a yarn ball winder is crucial for achieving optimal results and ensuring the longevity of both the winder and the yarn itself. Mastering these adjustments can greatly enhance the quality of the yarn balls and make the winding process smoother and more efficient.

The tension of a yarn ball winder refers to how tightly the yarn is wound around the core of the ball. Proper tension is essential because it affects not only the shape and compactness of the yarn ball but also the ease with which the yarn will be used later. If the tension is too loose, the yarn may tangle or snag when being pulled out. Conversely, if it is wound too tightly, it can stretch or deform the yarn, potentially altering its texture and strength.

To adjust the tension, start by locating the tension guide on your winder, which is typically a small screw or knob that can be turned to increase or decrease the tension. Begin with a medium setting and wind a small amount of yarn. Pause to check the firmness of the ball— it should be firm but not overly tight, and the yarn should not be so loose that it loses shape. Adjust the tension accordingly, making minor modifications until the desired firmness is achieved. It is important to note that different types of yarn may require different tension settings; for example, delicate yarns like silk or cashmere need a gentler tension to avoid damage, while sturdier yarns like wool can handle tighter tension.

Speed, on the other hand, refers to how quickly the winder operates. The speed at which you wind the yarn can impact both the tension and the overall effectiveness of the winding process. Most manual yarn ball winders allow the user to control the speed by hand, whereas electric winders might have speed settings.

When using a manual winder, maintain a steady, even pace. If you wind too quickly, the yarn may not catch properly, leading to uneven balls or worse, causing the yarn to snap. A slower speed ensures greater control and helps maintain consistent tension throughout the ball. For electric winders, start with the lowest speed setting and gradually increase as you become more comfortable with the winder's operation. Watching the yarn as it winds will help you determine the best speed—too fast and the yarn might stretch, too slow and the process becomes laborious.

In the context of learning how to use a yarn ball winder, understanding how to adjust the tension and speed is foundational. These adjustments are not just about handling the winder but about crafting a better end product. Winding yarn properly prepares it for use in projects, ensuring that it feeds smoothly and maintains its intended texture and strength during knitting or crocheting. Practicing these adjustments also helps users develop a feel for their tools and materials, which is a critical aspect of skilled craftsmanship in yarn arts.

Whether you are a beginner just starting out with a yarn ball winder or an experienced user looking to refine your technique, taking the time to learn about tension and speed adjustments will greatly improve your crafting experience. It empowers you to work more efficiently and produce consistently high-quality yarn balls, ultimately making your knitting or crocheting projects more enjoyable and successful.

Chapter: 4 Advanced Techniques

Winding Different Types of Yarns

Winding different types of yarns using a yarn ball winder involves understanding the unique characteristics of each yarn type and adjusting the winding technique accordingly. This knowledge ensures that the yarn is prepared in a way that enhances the crafting process, whether knitting, crocheting, or weaving.

Fiber Varieties and Their Impact on Winding

The first step in mastering advanced winding techniques is recognizing the diversity in yarn fibers. Natural fibers like wool, cotton, silk, and alpaca each have distinct properties that influence how they should be handled during winding. For instance, wool's elasticity requires a gentle touch to avoid stretching the fibers, whereas cotton, lacking this elasticity, can tolerate a firmer wind.

Synthetic fibers, such as acrylic and polyester, are generally more durable and less prone to breakage. However, they can also be slippery, making them challenging to wind tightly without slipping off the ball winder. Blended fibers combine the qualities of both natural and synthetic yarns, necessitating a balanced approach to winding.

Adjusting Tension for Different Yarns

The tension applied during the winding process is crucial for maintaining the integrity of the yarn. Too much tension can deform elastic fibers, while too little can result in loosely formed yarn balls that tangle easily. For delicate yarns like silk and fine alpaca, it's essential to use minimal tension, allowing the yarn to guide itself onto the winder almost effortlessly.

Bulkier yarns, such as chunky wool or thick cotton, require a moderate tension that helps in forming a more compact ball that is easier to store and use. The winder's tension setting, if adjustable, should be tested on a small amount of yarn before fully committing to winding an entire skein.

Dealing with Textured and Novelty Yarns

Textured yarns, including bouclé, chenille, or yarns with sequins and beads, pose additional challenges due to their uneven surfaces. These yarns should be wound slowly, with constant attention to prevent the yarn from catching or snagging. In some cases, winding by hand might be necessary to preserve the yarn's unique attributes.

Techniques for Avoiding Tangles and Snags

Before winding, inspect the yarn for knots or weak points. If knots are found, they should be untied or cut out, and the ends securely joined to avoid breaks during winding. For long-hair fibers or very fine yarns, using a yarn guide that controls the yarn's path can help in managing the flow onto the winder and prevent snags.

Winding from Skeins or Hanks

When winding yarn from skeins or hanks, it is important to first ensure that the yarn is free from twists and is properly secured. Using a swift in conjunction with the yarn ball winder can greatly enhance the ease and efficiency of this process. The swift holds the hank taut and spins freely as the winder pulls yarn, thereby preventing tangles and ensuring a smooth transition onto the winder.

Ensuring Yarn Readiness for Projects

The final step in winding different types of yarns is checking the yarn ball for readiness. This includes ensuring the outer end is accessible for immediate use and that the ball is not too tight, which could strain the fibers over time. For center-pull balls, it's important to secure the inner end so it doesn't slip back inside, which can cause internal tangles.

Mastering these advanced techniques for winding different types
of yarns enhances the crafting experience by preparing the yarn in
the most optimal form for use. Each type of yarn may require a
unique approach, but with practice and attention to detail, using
a yarn ball winder can become a vital part of efficient and
enjoyable yarn crafting.

Dealing with Knots and Tangles

Dealing with knots and tangles is an inevitable challenge for anyone who works with yarn. Fortunately, mastering the use of a yarn ball winder can significantly aid in managing and minimizing these frustrations. This advanced technique is crucial for maintaining the integrity of the yarn and ensuring a smooth crafting experience.

When beginning the winding process, it's important to start with careful preparation of the yarn. Before placing a skein onto the yarn ball winder, it should be inspected for any existing knots or weak points. If knots are found, gently untie them if possible or cut the yarn at the knot and carefully join the ends with a discreet knot that won't interfere with the winding or subsequent knitting or crocheting.

As you load the yarn onto the ball winder, pay attention to how it is unwinding. The yarn should come off the skein smoothly without resistance. One effective way to ensure this is to use a swift, an adjustable tool that holds the yarn skein taut and rotates as the winder pulls yarn from it. This setup helps prevent the yarn from tangling as it feeds into the ball winder. If you notice resistance or the formation of loops that could lead to knots, stop winding and address these issues immediately to prevent them from becoming more severe.

While winding, it's helpful to maintain a consistent tension. This doesn't mean pulling the yarn tight but rather keeping it sufficiently taut to ensure that it winds neatly onto the ball winder. This tension helps in forming a well-shaped yarn ball and reduces the chances of creating loops that can turn into tangles later. If the yarn does begin to tangle, pause the winding process. Gently pull the tangled section out to length and lay it flat to untangle by hand. This might seem time-consuming, but dealing with tangles early on can save much more time and prevent yarn waste in the long run.

Sometimes, despite best efforts, tangles can occur within the ball during winding. In such cases, it's usually because the yarn was already compromised before winding. When you encounter a tangle that cannot be untangled by simply pulling apart, use a pair of scissors to carefully cut the tangle out. Then, securely tie the ends together with a small, strong knot and resume winding. Ensure that the knot is small enough to pass through your needles or hook easily without snagging.

In addition to these practical steps, maintaining your yarn ball winder is also essential in preventing knots and tangles. Ensure that your winder is clean and free from dust and fiber build-up, which can catch the yarn and cause it to snag or tear. Periodically check the winder for any rough edges or areas where yarn might catch and address these issues promptly.

Using a yarn ball winder, when done correctly, not only helps in creating tidy, usable yarn balls but also plays a significant role in managing potential knots and tangles. This enhances your overall crafting efficiency and enjoyment, making your time spent with yarn more about creating and less about fixing problems. By integrating these techniques into your yarn preparation routine, you ensure that each crafting session can proceed as smoothly and enjoyably as possible.

Creating Center-Pull Yarn Balls

Creating center-pull yarn balls is a skill that can significantly enhance your crafting efficiency and enjoyment. This technique allows you to pull yarn smoothly from the center of the ball as you knit or crochet, preventing the ball from rolling away and decreasing the likelihood of tangles. When using a yarn ball winder, mastering the method of creating center-pull balls transforms a simple winding session into an advanced craft technique that contributes to a more organized and enjoyable crafting experience.

To begin, you'll need a yarn ball winder properly mounted and stabilized on a table or a similar flat surface. Ensure the winder is secure, as a stable winder is critical for creating evenly wound yarn balls. Start by finding the end of your yarn from the skein or hank. This end will eventually become the center-pull end.

Once you have located the end, thread it through the tension guide of the yarn ball winder if your model includes this feature. The tension guide helps maintain consistent tension on the yarn, which is crucial for creating a ball that unwinds smoothly without collapsing. After threading the yarn through the guide, pull a small amount of yarn and secure it in the notch at the top of the winder's spindle. This action marks the beginning of your center-pull capability.

As you start winding, turn the handle slowly and steadily. It's essential to maintain an even pace, as erratic winding can lead to uneven layers that might not pull smoothly when you're knitting or crocheting. As the yarn winds, it should begin forming a neat cake-shaped ball. The initial end you secured will gently be worked into the center of this cake.

During the winding process, keep an eye on the tension. If the yarn is too tight, it can stretch and distort, while yarn that's too loose may not form a stable ball. Adjust the tension as needed by modifying how you feed the yarn into the winder. For some types of yarn, especially slippery or delicate fibers, you might need to guide the yarn with your hand to prevent snags or uneven tension.

As the ball reaches your desired size, cut the yarn leaving a tail long enough to secure around the ball's outside, ensuring it doesn't unravel. Slowly remove the ball from the winder, being careful to locate the original end that was placed in the spindle's notch. This is your center-pull end.

For an extra touch of neatness and security, you can use a yarn sleeve or a small piece of yarn to tie around the finished ball. This action helps keep the outer end in place and maintains the ball's shape until you're ready to use it.

Using a yarn ball winder to create center-pull balls is not just a matter of convenience; it's a technique that, once mastered, can significantly enhance the functionality and pleasure of your crafting sessions. It ensures that your yarn stays clean and organized, reducing frustration and allowing you to focus more on the creative aspects of your projects. The knowledge and ability to create center-pull yarn balls also underscore a deeper understanding of your tools and materials, an essential aspect of becoming a proficient knitter or crocheter.

Chapter: 5 Maintenance and Troubleshooting

Cleaning Your Yarn Ball Winder

Maintaining a yarn ball winder involves regular cleaning and care to ensure it continues to function effectively and extends its lifespan. When it comes to cleaning your yarn ball winder, it's important to follow a methodical approach that not only keeps the tool in good working condition but also helps prevent common issues that can arise from neglect.

The process begins with the disassembly of the yarn ball winder, if possible. Before proceeding, consult the manufacturer's manual to understand which parts can be safely removed and cleaned separately. Typically, this includes removable spindles or winding arms. By disassembling the parts that come into direct contact with the yarn, you can access areas where lint, dust, and yarn fibers tend to accumulate.

Once the winder is disassembled, use a soft, dry cloth to wipe down each component. Avoid using water or chemical cleaners unless specified by the manufacturer, as these can damage the materials used in the winder, such as plastic or wood. For those hard-to-reach areas, a can of compressed air can be very effective in removing dust and lint. Alternatively, a small, soft-bristled brush, like a toothbrush, can dislodge any debris stuck in the crevices of each part.

In addition to physical cleaning, it's crucial to check for any signs of wear or damage, such as cracks or loose parts. Tighten any screws that may have become loose during use, and if any parts appear worn out or broken, consult with the manufacturer for replacement parts. Regular inspection and replacement of worn components are vital in preventing malfunctions during operation.

Lubrication is another key aspect of maintaining a yarn ball winder. Some models may require a light application of machine oil to keep the moving parts operating smoothly. Apply oil sparingly to areas such as the gears or any metal-on-metal contact points. It's important to use only the type of oil recommended by the manufacturer to avoid damaging the parts or leaving unwanted residue on the yarn.

After cleaning and lubricating, reassemble the yarn ball winder, making sure all parts are securely in place. Test the winder with a small amount of yarn to ensure everything is working as it should. This test run will help identify any issues with tension or alignment that may have arisen from improper reassembly.

When troubleshooting common issues with a yarn ball winder, start by checking for obvious problems like tangled yarn or incorrect setup. If the winder is not turning smoothly, check for obstructions or excess lint build-up. Should the winder produce uneven yarn balls, re-evaluate the tension settings and adjust according to the yarn type and desired tightness.

For those who use their yarn ball winder frequently, it is advisable to perform a thorough cleaning and maintenance check every few months. This routine not only preserves the functionality of the winder but also ensures that every yarn ball wound is neat and ready for use.

By understanding how to properly clean and maintain a yarn ball winder, users can significantly enhance their crafting experience, making the process smoother and more enjoyable. Regular maintenance not only solves and prevents operational issues but also instills a sense of confidence and satisfaction in the use of the tool, making it an indispensable part of the crafting process.

Common Issues and How to Solve Them

When it comes to using a yarn ball winder, several common issues might arise that can hinder the device's efficiency and the quality of the yarn balls it produces. Recognizing these issues and knowing how to troubleshoot them can help crafters maintain their equipment in optimal condition, ensuring a smooth and enjoyable crafting experience.

Tangled Yarn is one of the most frequent problems encountered. This often occurs if the yarn is not properly threaded through the tension guide or if the winder is operated at an inconsistent speed. To solve this, ensure the yarn feeds smoothly through all guides without obstruction and maintain a steady pace when winding. If tangles continue, inspect the yarn path for any rough spots or debris that might be catching the yarn.

Unevenly Wound Balls are another issue, which can result from uneven tension or speed during the winding process. Make sure the yarn winder is securely fastened to a stable surface and that the tension guide is adjusted to the appropriate tightness for the yarn weight. Operating the winder at a consistent speed also helps in forming even layers across the ball.

Overstretched Yarn can occur if the tension is too tight, affecting the yarn's elasticity and texture. This is especially problematic for natural fibers like wool, which can become permanently deformed. To avoid this, adjust the tension settings to a lower level and test on a small amount of yarn before winding the entire skein. It's vital to find a balance where the yarn is neither too loose (causing tangles) nor too tight (causing stretching).

Noisy Operation might indicate mechanical issues with the winder. Often, this is due to lack of lubrication or accumulated dust and fiber within the gears. Regularly clean the winder with a soft brush or cloth to remove debris. Apply a light lubricant specifically designed for small gears if the noise persists, ensuring it's suitable for use near yarn to avoid any potential damage or staining.

Slipping or Misalignment of the yarn ball on the spindle may occur if the spindle is worn out or if the winder's clamp isn't tight enough. Check that the winder is clamped securely to a flat, stable surface. If the spindle shows signs of wear, such as visible grooves or uneven surfaces, consider replacing this part to ensure proper functionality.

Handle Problems such as stiffness or difficulty in turning can usually be traced back to internal issues with the gears or handle assembly. First, check for any visible obstructions or dirt build-up that could be causing friction. If the handle continues to be difficult to turn, dismantle the handle assembly according to the manufacturer's instructions, clean all parts, and reassemble. Sometimes, replacement of worn-out parts is necessary.

Breaking Yarn might happen if there are sharp edges along the yarn path or if the tension is too high. Examine the yarn winder for any damage or rough edges around the yarn guide or spindle. Smooth these areas with fine sandpaper if needed. Always ensure that the yarn tension is appropriate for the type of yarn being wound, adjusting as necessary to prevent undue stress on the yarn.

Proper maintenance and troubleshooting of a yarn ball winder not only extend the lifespan of the tool but also improve the quality of work a crafter can produce. Regular checks, cleaning, and adjustments ensure that the winder operates smoothly, thereby enhancing the overall crafting experience. By familiarizing themselves with common issues and solutions, users of yarn ball winders can efficiently manage any challenges that arise, keeping their focus on the joys of yarn crafting.

When to Seek Professional Help

When using a yarn ball winder, encountering occasional issues with maintenance and operation is common, and many of these can be addressed with basic troubleshooting techniques. However, there are circumstances where professional help becomes necessary to ensure the longevity and proper functioning of the device. Recognizing when to transition from DIY fixes to professional assistance can save both time and the risk of further damaging the winder.

The first scenario in which professional help is advisable is when there is evident mechanical failure. If the yarn ball winder stops functioning altogether—such as the crank not turning or the winder not winding despite proper setup and handling—internal mechanisms may be at fault. This could be due to broken gears, a malfunctioning spindle, or other critical components that are not easily accessible or repairable without specific tools and expertise.

Another indication for seeking professional assistance is when there are persistent issues with yarn tension and quality of the wound balls despite following the manufacturer's guidelines and troubleshooting advice. If the balls are consistently too loose, too tight, or unevenly wound, it might point to a calibration issue or a problem with the tension arm or winding mechanism. Professionals can adjust or replace these components accurately, which is crucial for the winder to operate correctly.

Persistent noise during operation is also a sign that professional servicing might be required. While some noise is normal, any sudden changes such as grinding, clicking, or thumping sounds suggest internal problems. These noises could indicate loose or worn-out parts that, if left unchecked, could lead to complete failure of the winder.

Electrical issues in motorized yarn ball winders are particularly complex. Signs such as intermittent stopping, failure to start, or electrical smells are critical and require immediate attention from a professional. DIY electrical repairs can be dangerous and might violate product warranties or safety regulations.

Professional help should also be considered if there are visible signs of wear and tear that affect the functionality of the winder. Components like the winding arm, guide ring, or the base might show excessive wear or damage after prolonged use. Replacement and proper installation of these parts are often best handled by professionals who can ensure that the winder remains stable and functional.

Moreover, if the yarn ball winder is still under warranty, it is advisable to contact the manufacturer or an authorized service center for any issues. Unauthorized repairs can void warranties and potentially lead to greater costs down the line.

In summary, while many minor issues with a yarn ball winder can be solved at home, recognizing the signs that indicate a need for professional intervention is crucial. Mechanical failures, persistent functional issues, unusual noises, electrical problems, and significant wear and tear are all valid reasons to seek professional help. Doing so ensures that the yarn ball winder can continue to be a valuable, efficient, and safe tool in your crafting arsenal.

Chapter: 6 Creative Uses for Your Yarn Ball Winder

Beyond Yarn: Other Materials You Can Wind

Exploring the capabilities of a yarn ball winder extends well beyond its traditional use with yarn. This versatile tool can be adapted to handle a variety of other materials, broadening the scope of projects and applications for crafters, organizers, and even small business owners. Here's a look at how you can use a yarn ball winder with other materials and the creative possibilities each offers.

One intriguing material that can be wound using a yarn ball winder is ribbon. Whether for crafting, gift wrapping, or decorating, ribbons can be neatly wound into compact rolls. This not only prevents tangling and creasing but also makes it easier to measure and cut the lengths needed for projects. By maintaining an organized ribbon collection, crafters can quickly select the best color and style for any occasion, streamlining the creation of bows, garlands, or decorative accents.

Embroidery floss is another excellent candidate for winding. Typically used for cross-stitch, embroidery, or friendship bracelets, floss can easily become a tangled mess. Winding embroidery floss onto small bobbins using a yarn ball winder creates a neat, organized system. This system not only preserves the quality of the floss but also simplifies the process of switching between colors during intricate projects.

Fishing line, often unruly and prone to tangling, can also be managed effectively with a yarn ball winder. Anglers can use the winder to prepare and store multiple types of lines, keeping them ready for quick changes while on the water. This can be particularly useful for organizing different weights and lengths, ensuring that lines are accessible and in good condition, thereby enhancing the fishing experience.

For gardeners, thin wire or twine used for training plants or marking rows can be wound using a yarn ball winder. This helps keep gardening supplies tidy and ready to use, preventing the all-too-common tangling that occurs in tool sheds and boxes. Garden twine wound into a ball also becomes more portable and easier to handle, making outdoor tasks more efficient.

In the realm of textiles and fabric arts, strips of fabric used in quilting or rug-making can also be wound into neat rolls. This makes storage and usage more manageable, especially for those who work with multiple colors and patterns. Having pre-cut, pre-wound strips allows for quicker selection and can inspire creative pattern making.

Additionally, for those interested in crafting or home décor, cords such as those used for macramé or decorative lighting can be wound with a yarn ball winder. This makes the cords easier to measure, cut, and manipulate, which is particularly handy when working on large projects like wall hangings or custom light installations.

Beyond crafting and domestic use, small business owners who deal with materials like cables, wires, or small hoses can benefit from the organizational capabilities of a yarn ball winder. In electronics, automotive, or computer repair shops, having neatly wound cables can streamline operations and reduce workspace clutter, thereby increasing efficiency and reducing setup and cleanup time.

Using a yarn ball winder for these various materials not only helps in maintaining an organized workspace but also enhances productivity and creativity. It's about transforming a simple tool into a multi-purpose asset that can tackle a range of materials, each bringing its own set of challenges and rewards. This expanded use of a yarn ball winder also emphasizes the versatility and value of understanding and mastering this tool, as outlined in "How to Use a Yarn Ball Winder," providing users with more ways to optimize their crafts and daily tasks.

Projects That Benefit from Evenly Wound Yarn Balls

In the realm of yarn crafts, the importance of preparation cannot be overstated, and one key aspect of this preparation is the use of a yarn ball winder to create evenly wound yarn balls. This simple step can make a substantial difference in the execution and outcome of various projects. Whether engaging in knitting, crocheting, or other yarn-based crafts, evenly wound yarn balls ensure a smoother, more efficient workflow and a superior final product.

For knitters, projects like intricate lacework, where consistent tension and yarn flow are crucial, benefit immensely from evenly wound yarn balls. Lace patterns require precise stitch counts and tension to maintain their delicate, openwork appearance. Any inconsistencies in yarn tension can lead to uneven stitches that mar the beauty and structure of the lace. Similarly, colorwork in knitting, such as Fair Isle or intarsia, can be made easier with the use of a yarn ball winder. Managing multiple colors of yarn becomes more manageable when each color is wound into a neat ball, reducing the likelihood of the yarns tangling. This can help maintain a clean, crisp transition between colors without the frustration of knots or yarn barf.

Crocheters, too, find that projects like amigurumi—small, stuffed yarn creatures that require tight, consistent stitches—turn out much better when using yarn that has been wound into tight, center-pull balls. The consistent tension helps maintain the right gauge and makes the finished product look polished and professional. Additionally, large projects such as blankets or throws also benefit from evenly wound yarn balls. These projects often require significant amounts of yarn, and having them wound into balls enables easy handling and storage, making it convenient to pick up the work at any time without dealing with knots or tangles.

Beyond knitting and crocheting, other crafts can also utilize a yarn ball winder for enhanced results. Weavers can use evenly wound yarn for their warps and wefts, ensuring smooth feeding through the loom and consistent tension across their creations. This is especially important when creating items where structural integrity and evenness are key, such as fabrics for clothing or home décor. In a more unconventional sense, artists who use yarn in mixed media art find that pre-wound balls allow them to better estimate and segment their usage, creating intricate yarn art without wastage or guesswork.

Furthermore, crafters who enjoy making tassels, pom-poms, or other decorative elements find that a yarn ball winder can be a practical tool in their crafting arsenal. By winding yarn into uniform balls, crafters can ensure that each decorative piece is consistent in size and density, which is essential for projects requiring symmetrical and uniform decorations.

In crafting, the joy often lies in the process as much as in the final product, and having tools that make the process as seamless and enjoyable as possible can greatly enhance this experience. A yarn ball winder, while seemingly simple, supports this by ensuring that yarn is easy to manage, reducing setup time, and letting crafters focus more on the creative aspects of their projects. Whether the project is small and intricate or large and demanding, the foundational step of preparing yarn with a ball winder sets the stage for a successful and enjoyable crafting endeavor.

Chapter: 7 Comparing Yarn Ball Winders

Manual vs. Electric Yarn Ball Winders

When selecting a yarn ball winder, crafters have the choice between manual and electric models, each with its distinct features and benefits. This choice plays a critical role in the efficiency, ease of use, and suitability of the tool for specific projects and environments.

Manual yarn ball winders are the more traditional type, operated by a crank that the user turns by hand. The simplicity of this design is one of its greatest advantages. Manual winders are typically more affordable and portable, requiring no power source, which makes them ideal for crafters who prefer a mobile or more tactile approach to their crafting setup. They tend to be smaller and easier to store, an important consideration for those with limited space. Additionally, the manual operation allows for greater control over the speed and tension of winding, which can be crucial when dealing with delicate or uniquely textured yarns.

However, manual winders can be somewhat labor-intensive, especially for those who wind large quantities of yarn regularly. The physical effort required to operate the crank can be a drawback, particularly for users with hand or wrist issues. Furthermore, the speed at which yarn can be wound with a manual model is inherently slower and depends on the user's physical speed and stamina.

Electric yarn ball winders, on the other hand, offer convenience and speed that manual models cannot match. These devices are powered by a motor, eliminating the need for manual cranking. With the push of a button, the winder can process yarn much faster than a manual winder, a significant advantage for high-volume users or professionals. Electric winders can handle larger quantities and often accommodate heavier yarns with greater ease. This reduces the time and effort involved in preparation, allowing crafters to focus more on their creative work.

The increased power and speed of electric winders do come with some considerations. They are generally more expensive than manual models, representing a higher initial investment. They also require a power source, which can limit their portability and the settings in which they can be used. While they offer speed, the motor's force can sometimes be too harsh for extremely delicate yarns, potentially causing snags or damage if not carefully monitored.

When choosing between a manual and an electric yarn ball winder, crafters should consider their specific needs. For those who value portability, have a tight budget, or enjoy the hands-on control of winding yarn, a manual winder may be the best choice. For those who produce large volumes of yarn balls, value efficiency over manual control, or have physical limitations that make manual winding difficult, an electric winder is likely the more suitable option.

In relation to learning "How to Use a Yarn Ball Winder," understanding the differences between manual and electric models is crucial. Each type requires different setups, operational techniques, and maintenance routines. Knowing whether a manual or electric winder best suits one's needs will influence how effectively one can utilize the winder, impacting the overall efficiency and enjoyment of the crafting process. Thus, choosing the right type of yarn ball winder is not just a matter of preference but a strategic decision that can significantly affect a crafter's productivity and satisfaction with their projects.

Best Practices for Both Types

When comparing yarn ball winders, it's essential to understand that both manual and electric models have their unique sets of best practices to ensure optimal performance and longevity. These guidelines help crafters make the most out of whichever type of winder they choose, contributing to a more efficient and enjoyable crafting experience.

Manual Yarn Ball Winders

Manual yarn ball winders are beloved for their simplicity and portability. These devices require no power source other than manual effort, making them perfect for crafters who prefer a hands-on approach or need a tool that can be used anywhere, anytime.

1. **Placement and Stability**: Always secure the manual winder firmly to a sturdy, flat surface. Most manual winders come with a clamp or similar securing mechanism. Ensuring the winder is stable before use is crucial to prevent it from moving or tipping while in operation, which can affect the yarn's tension and potentially damage the winder or the yarn.

2. **Even Tension**: While winding, maintain a consistent tension on the yarn. This prevents the yarn from becoming too loose or too tight, which can cause uneven balls or strain the winder. The

tension should be enough to feed the yarn smoothly into the winder without pulling it taut.

3. **Pace Yourself**: Because manual winders rely on physical effort, it's important to wind at a steady, moderate pace to avoid wear on the device and fatigue on the part of the user. A rhythmical, consistent speed yields the best results.

4. **Regular Maintenance**: Keep the winder clean from lint and yarn fibers, which can build up and affect its performance. Occasionally check all moving parts and the clamping mechanism to ensure they're working correctly and haven't loosened over time.

Electric Yarn Ball Winders

Electric yarn ball winders offer speed and ease of use, especially valuable for those who wind large quantities of yarn regularly. They require less manual effort and can handle a wider range of yarn weights and lengths effortlessly.

1. **Power Source and Setup**: Always ensure that your electric winder is connected to a compatible power source and that all electrical connections are secure and undamaged. Set up the winder on a stable, level surface where it can operate without interference.

2. **Speed Settings**: Familiarize yourself with the speed settings of your electric winder. Different yarns may require different winding speeds to avoid breaking delicate yarns or failing to wind thicker ones tightly enough. Starting at a lower speed and gradually increasing as needed can help find the optimal setting for each yarn type.

3. **Monitoring**: Unlike manual winders, electric models can sometimes feed yarn very quickly. It's important to monitor the winding process closely to catch any potential issues early, such as yarn snags or uneven winding. Immediate intervention can prevent damage to both the yarn and the winder.

4. **Lubrication and Maintenance**: Depending on the model, some electric winders might require periodic lubrication of moving parts to keep them running smoothly. Always refer to the manufacturer's guidelines for specific maintenance routines and stick to them diligently.

For both types of yarn ball winders, understanding and respecting the tool's capabilities and limits is vital. Avoid overloading the winder with yarn weights or amounts that exceed what the manufacturer recommends. Regularly inspect your winder for wear and tear, especially after extended use or when switching between different types of yarn. By adhering to these best practices, crafters can significantly enhance their experience, whether they choose a manual or an electric yarn ball winder.

This knowledge not only aids in achieving the best results in yarn preparation but also extends the life of the tool, ensuring it remains a valuable part of the crafting process for years to come.

Product Reviews and Recommendations

When diving into the world of yarn crafts, choosing the right tools can make all the difference in your creative endeavors. A yarn ball winder is one such essential tool, and understanding the nuances between different models can help crafters select the best option for their needs. Here we will explore various yarn ball winder products, highlighting their unique features, performance, and user feedback to guide crafters in making informed decisions.

The market offers a range of yarn ball winders, from basic manual models to more advanced electric ones. Each type suits different levels of usage, from occasional hobbyists to professional artisans. Let's break down some popular models:

Manual Yarn Ball Winders:
Manual winders are typically more affordable and are great for those who knit or crochet as a hobby. They require manual operation, usually involving a crank handle.

1. Knit Picks Yarn Ball Winder - This is a compact, sturdy winder that can handle up to 100 grams of yarn at a time, suitable for those who work with standard yarn weights. Users appreciate its easy assembly and smooth operation, making it a favorite among beginners.

2. Stanwood Needlecraft Large Metal Winder - For those who need a bit more robustness, the Stanwood model can wind up to 10 oz of yarn, making it ideal for those working with bulkier yarns. It is noted for its durability and stability, thanks to its heavy-duty construction and metal gears.

Electric Yarn Ball Winders:
Electric yarn ball winders are excellent for those who need to wind large quantities of yarn quickly and with minimal effort, perfect for frequent users or small business owners.

1. **Boye Electric Yarn Ball Winder** - This electric winder is a time-saver, capable of winding balls quickly. It's particularly useful for those with joint pain or reduced hand strength. However, some users report it can be a bit noisy and may occasionally overheat with extensive use.

2. **Lacis Jumbo Yarn Ball Winder** - Designed for heavy-duty use, this model can handle up to 1 lb of yarn at a time. It's robust and reliable, with a price point reflecting its professional-grade capabilities. Users love its long-lasting build and efficiency, though its size might be cumbersome for smaller spaces.

User Experiences and Recommendations:
Feedback from users suggests a few common considerations when choosing a yarn ball winder:

- **Capacity** - Consider how much yarn you typically use. Larger capacities save time but require more storage space.
- **Durability** - Metal winders tend to last longer and withstand heavier use compared to their plastic counterparts.
- **Ease of Use** - Look for a model that sets up easily and operates smoothly without too much noise or vibration.
- **Price vs. Usage** - Determine how often you will use the winder. Occasional crafters might opt for a simpler, more cost-effective model, while frequent users might invest in a higher-end product.

When integrating the yarn ball winder into your crafting routine, the "How to Use a Yarn Ball Winder" guidance proves invaluable. This knowledge allows crafters to fully leverage their chosen winder's capabilities, enhancing their overall crafting experience by ensuring smooth, efficient yarn preparation. Whether you opt for a manual or an electric model, the right yarn ball winder can significantly streamline your projects, letting you focus more on creativity and less on preparation.

Chapter: 8 Resources for Further Learning

Recommended Reading and Videos

Exploring resources for further learning about how to use a yarn ball winder can immensely enhance one's understanding and proficiency in using this invaluable crafting tool. There are a variety of books, online articles, and video tutorials that cater to both beginners and advanced users, providing detailed instructions, tips, and creative ideas for getting the most out of a yarn ball winder.

For those who prefer a structured approach to learning, several books offer comprehensive insights into not only the mechanics of using a yarn ball winder but also the broader context of yarn crafting. A standout recommendation is "The Complete Guide to Yarn Winding," which covers everything from the basics of setting up and operating different types of winders to advanced techniques for handling tricky yarns. The book also delves into maintenance tips to keep the winder in optimal condition and troubleshooting common problems that users may encounter.

Another excellent resource is "Yarn Crafting: Tools and Techniques," which dedicates an entire chapter to yarn ball winders. This chapter provides a deep dive into selecting the right winder for specific yarn types and project needs, illustrated with high-quality photos and step-by-step guides that make learning easy and enjoyable.

Online platforms offer a treasure trove of video tutorials that are particularly useful for visual learners. YouTube channels such as "Knit Mastery" and "Crochet Corner" regularly feature demonstrations on using yarn ball winders. These videos often include live demonstrations of winding different types of yarn, from standard wool to more complex fibers like silk or bamboo. Viewers can see firsthand how to adjust tension, correct uneven winding, and integrate the use of a winder into larger project workflows.

For those interested in the technical aspects of yarn ball winders, the video series "Mechanics of Yarn Winding" on Vimeo offers a more in-depth look at the engineering and mechanics behind the tool. These videos are ideal for users who not only want to use their winders effectively but also understand how they can repair and modify them to suit specific needs.

Blogs and online articles also serve as fantastic resources. Sites like Craftsy and Ravelry feature articles written by seasoned knitters and crocheters who share their personal tips and tricks for using yarn ball winders. These articles often include product reviews, comparisons between manual and electric models, and advice on integrating winders into various crafting projects.

For a more interactive learning experience, many online crafting communities host webinars and live Q&A sessions where experts demonstrate the use of yarn ball winders and answer viewer questions in real time. These sessions provide an opportunity to learn from the experiences of a diverse group of crafters and to receive personalized advice.

In addition to these resources, attending workshops or classes at local craft stores or through community education programs can provide hands-on experience with guidance from experienced instructors. These classes often cover yarn ball winder basics along with other crafting tools, making them a well-rounded educational opportunity.

By engaging with these recommended readings and videos, crafters can not only master the basic use of a yarn ball winder but also explore its creative applications, ensuring that this tool becomes a cornerstone of their crafting toolkit.

Online Communities and Support

Engaging with online communities and accessing digital support resources can greatly enhance the learning experience for those looking to master the use of a yarn ball winder. These platforms offer a wealth of information, from basic tutorials to advanced troubleshooting tips, helping individuals of all skill levels to refine their techniques and solve any issues they might encounter.

One of the most accessible resources is online forums dedicated to knitting and crocheting. These forums often have specific threads where experienced crafters share their knowledge about different tools, including yarn ball winders. New users can find detailed posts on how to set up their winder, the best practices for winding different types of yarn, and solutions to common problems. For instance, a user struggling with uneven tension might find a step-by-step guide on adjusting their technique, tailored advice from community members, or even video links that demonstrate the process visually.

Video tutorial platforms, such as YouTube, serve as another vital resource. Many crafters and bloggers post comprehensive videos that not only show the winder in action but also discuss its features, benefits, and maintenance tips. These videos often include reviews of different brands and models, which can be extremely helpful for someone in the market for their first yarn ball winder or looking to upgrade their current setup. Watching a seasoned crafter use the tool can provide insights that are sometimes missed in written instructions, such as the angle at which to feed the yarn into the winder to avoid snags and breaks.

Social media groups, especially those on platforms like Facebook and Instagram, also contribute significantly to the learning curve. Members of these groups frequently share photos and videos of their setups, offer DIY solutions to enhance the functionality of their winders, and provide emotional and technical support to each other. These communities are often very welcoming and eager to help newcomers, providing a sense of belonging and mutual support.

Blogs written by knitting and crocheting enthusiasts are a treasure trove of information as well. Bloggers often publish in-depth reviews, troubleshooting guides, and even hacks for optimizing the use of a yarn ball winder. Some might offer downloadable resources, like checklists or maintenance schedules, which can be particularly useful for keeping a winder in good working condition.

Finally, manufacturer websites should not be overlooked. Many manufacturers provide FAQs, user manuals, and direct customer support. Some even host their own user forums or have a customer service chat feature. These resources are invaluable for troubleshooting specific models, understanding warranty options, and obtaining spare parts if necessary.

For someone learning how to use a yarn ball winder, tapping into these online resources and communities can significantly ease the learning process. The collective knowledge and experience found in these digital spaces not only help in resolving practical issues but also enhance the overall crafting experience by connecting individuals with a global network of like-minded enthusiasts. Whether it's finding the right way to thread a delicate yarn without breakage or discovering creative ways to organize wound yarn balls, the support and inspiration are just a few clicks away.

Conclusion

As the exploration of the yarn ball winder draws to a close, the numerous advantages and methodologies associated with this tool crystallize into a compelling narrative of improved efficiency, creativity, and satisfaction in yarn crafts. The yarn ball winder, initially just a mechanical device, emerges as an indispensable ally in the transformation of unwieldy skeins into neat, ready-to-use balls of yarn. This change not only facilitates a more organized and efficient workflow but also enhances the overall enjoyment and outcome of knitting and crocheting projects.

Understanding the full range of the yarn ball winder's capabilities through detailed instruction on its setup, operation, and maintenance translates into a significant time-saving and reduction in manual labor for crafters. With the ability to quickly wind yarn into uniform balls, crafters can avoid the common pitfalls of tangling and can maintain consistent tension in their work, which is crucial for achieving professional-quality results. This level of consistency is especially beneficial in projects that require multiple balls of yarn, where variations in yarn tension or quality can visibly affect the final product.

Moreover, the yarn ball winder's importance extends beyond its functional benefits. It represents a shift towards a more thoughtful and efficient approach to crafting, where every aspect of the process is optimized for maximum productivity and enjoyment. This tool not only serves practical purposes but also encourages crafters to engage more deeply with their craft, understanding the intricacies of their materials and the tools they use.

Additionally, the discussions about the yarn ball winder invariably lead to an appreciation for the broader community of crafters. Online forums, tutorial videos, and social media groups not only provide practical advice and support but also foster a sense of community and shared passion. This communal aspect can be particularly comforting and inspiring for both novice and experienced crafters, as they navigate the various challenges and joys of yarn crafting.

In summary, the journey through learning how to use a yarn ball winder is about much more than mastering a tool; it's about enhancing one's crafting practice in every dimension. From saving time and reducing frustration to connecting with a global community of fellow enthusiasts, the benefits of using a yarn ball winder touch every aspect of the crafting experience. Thus, armed with this knowledge, crafters are better positioned to elevate their craft, making their creative endeavors not only more productive but also more enjoyable. This conclusion serves not just as an endpoint but as a gateway to new possibilities in the world of yarn crafting, where efficiency and enjoyment go hand in hand.

9 798323 218516